HOME
ECONOMICS
CAREERS

HOME ECONOMICS CAREERS

by Gilda Berger

FRANKLIN WATTS | NEW YORK | LONDON | 1977

Photographs courtesy of: Montefiore Hospital and Medical Center: pp. 3, 22, 30; Parsons School of Design: pp. 8, 35, 43; U.S.D.A. Extension Service: pp. 12, 14; Department of Housing and Urban Development: pp. 27, 51, 56; International Ladies' Garment Workers' Union: pp. 37, 38; The Sheraton Corporation: p. 49.

Library of Congress Cataloging in Publication Data

Berger, Gilda.
    Home economics careers.

    (Career concise guides)
    Includes index.
    SUMMARY: Discusses a career in home economics, the various specializations in the field, and the requirements and salary potential of each.
    1. Home economics—Vocational guidance—Juvenile literature. [1. Home economics—Vocational guidance. 2. Vocational guidance] I. Title
TX164.B47   640'.23   77–837
ISBN 0–531–01280–8

Contents

Home Economics:
An Introduction

Home economics is a people-helping field. It includes many careers that help people to eat better, dress better, and live better. Workers in the field teach and advise others on how to select and prepare food, furnish their homes, buy their clothes, protect their health, raise their children, manage their money, and make intelligent choices as consumers. If you have a special interest in any of these areas related to helping people, you can find a meaningful, satisfying career in home economics.

Are you interested in home economics education? About half the graduates in home economics become teachers. As a teacher in junior or senior high school, you help your students develop an understanding of the basic concepts of home economics. You show them how to apply their training to improve their own lives, and the lives of others. College home economics teachers give more advanced instruction in the concepts and skills of home economics, train students to become teachers, and do research. With a background in home economics education, you can also find worthwhile careers in consumer education and with the Extension Service.

Are you interested in child development and family relations? As a home economist with a background in this special area, with a teaching certificate you may teach children in a nursery school, Head Start program, day-care center, or a kindergarten. Or, you might be involved with children in a school for exceptional children. Your work might take you to rural or urban areas, either here or abroad, to work with the poor, the uneducated, and the culturally deprived. Your services might involve setting up a self-help program for needy families or individuals through a government agency, a private agency, or a community group.

Are you interested in food and nutrition? You can provide information about good eating habits and diet through a public health department, a medical center, or the Peace Corps. The same background might prepare you for a job as a food scientist who develops and analyzes food products in a food-processing plant or a research laboratory. Or, you can actually plan menus and supervise a kitchen where food is prepared for large numbers of people, such as in a hospital, school, nursing home, or other large institution.

Are you interested in clothing and textiles? If you specialize in this area, you can use your knowledge of fabrics, colors, and styles to work for a fabric or cloth-

**One of the vital areas
in home economics
is food and nutrition.**

[2

ing manufacturer, an advertising agency or a retail store. You can become a fashion designer, commentator, writer, or photographer. You can arrange fashion displays and exhibitions. You can work at cutting, sewing, fitting, or finishing articles of clothing. Or, you can inform homemakers on how to stretch their clothing dollar, and advise people on the wise selection and care of clothing.

Are you interested in housing, home furnishings, and equipment? A home economist who majors in housing, home furnishings, and equipment can find a variety of jobs in real estate firms, fabric or furniture manufacturers, or retail businesses. These jobs vary all the way from designing and testing appliances for the home, to presenting these products to the public. You can also select and arrange practical and efficient furnishings and decorations for homes, businesses, and institutions. And you can evaluate electrical, mechanical, and other types of housing equipment.

Are you interested in family finance and home management? As an expert on family finance and home management, you can give advice on how to prepare a budget, and how to balance income and expenses to achieve financial stability and security. You can help people make intelligent purchases of goods and services, and to understand their rights as consumers. Working in a government agency, or a bank, finance corporation, or insurance company, can give you opportunities to help people meet economic emergencies and make financial decisions.

There are well over 100,000 professional home economists in the United States and Canada. They hold bachelor's degrees, or advanced degrees such as a master's or Doctor of Philosophy from colleges that offer home economics as a major field of study. Working with them are many thousands more people, called paraprofessionals, who do not have college degrees. Most paraprofessionals are high school graduates who took courses in home economics. A number of paraprofessionals went to vocational training school or received on-the-job training.

If you are interested in a career as a professional in home economics, you will take the required basic college courses in home economics, as well as specialized courses in one area, such as food and nutrition, textiles and clothing, child development, or family relations. In addition, you will take courses in the sciences (biology, chemistry, physics), the arts (art, design, advertising), and the humanities (English, history, psychology).

Home economics is a living, growing, ever-changing field. There are more jobs available than there are people to fill them. There are many openings for highly trained professionals, as well as for paraprofessionals. Until recently, it was a field entered mostly by women. Now, however, as the number of job opportunities increases, and as men assume some of the responsibilities of homemaking, more men are taking on positions in the major areas of home economics.

Men and women in large numbers are now entering such new areas in home economics as marriage and family counseling, food production, administration of large institutions, consumer protection, rehabilitation of the physically, mentally, or culturally handicapped, or scientific research.

Each chapter in this book gives you a close-up look at a particular area in the field of home economics. The different sections within each chapter will help you decide if you are fitted for a career in that field.

As you read about the careers and jobs in home economics, try to imagine yourself in these positions and ask yourself these questions: Do I like the day-to-day tasks in this field? Do I have the abilities and personality that are required? Am I willing—and able—to get the education and experience that are needed for this career?

Then, ask yourself the most important question: Is a career in home economics for me?

Home Economics Education

Home economics educators help young people and adults to discover the hows and whys of homemaking. Homemakers today need to know what clothing to buy, which foods to eat, how to care for children, how to budget the family income, how to clean the house with a minimum of time and effort, where to live and how to furnish a house, and much, much more. Home economics educators also prepare people to teach these skills to others. The comfort and well-being of our families and homes depend on how well these subjects are taught and learned.

THE CAREER:
JUNIOR AND SENIOR
HIGH SCHOOL TEACHER

More home economists teach in junior and senior high schools than are employed in any other home economics profession. These home economics teachers work with students in every area of home economics study.

Home economics teachers often sponsor an FHA (Future Homemakers of America) club in their school. They provide many different activities and programs to help young people who are interested in home economics to expand their skills and interests.

But most home economics teachers do more than merely transmit knowledge and teach skills. Often they counsel teen-agers on personal problems and help students to prepare for jobs. The informal atmosphere in most home economics classrooms, and the personal nature of the subject matter, affords many opportunities for the teachers and students to exchange ideas, discuss problems, and seek solutions. Good home economics teachers do not impose their ideas on their students. They help students to make the decisions that will let them get value and meaning from their lives and improve the quality of life for others.

Try It Out

Prepare a short talk on Home Economics—Education for Life, to be given before a class in school. Mention the special interest areas of home economics. Tell specific ways that home economics educators prepare students to become better homemakers, parents, consumers, members of the community, and working people. Illustrate your talk with a chart that shows the six most important divisions of home economics, and two or three topics taught in each area.

**This student is learning
to perfect her
sewing and design skills.**

THE CAREER:
COLLEGE AND
UNIVERSITY TEACHER

The main job of the college or university home economics teacher is to prepare students for home economics teaching positions on all levels of education. College teachers are specialists in one or more of the fields of home economics. They give advanced instruction in the skills of home economics, as well as in the methods of teaching home economics. Some, who are education specialists, are asked to supervise student teachers who are getting teaching experience in actual classrooms under the guidance of experienced teachers. In addition to their classroom teaching, many college teachers also lecture, publish informational materials, and appear on radio and TV. In this way they are able to educate many more than just those who are taking their college courses.

Research is a very important part of the work of most college home economics teachers. They work in research laboratories and test kitchens in their universities, in government agencies, or in private industry. They look into all aspects of home economics: Do people who take large doses of vitamin C catch fewer colds? Do smooth- or rough-textured fabrics wear better? How do you judge the quality of a nursery school? Is a gas stove or an electric stove cheaper to operate? What is the ideal amount of life insurance to carry at various stages of life? How does the water temperature affect the cleansing power of a washing machine?

Their research findings are widely read and carry a great deal of influence. Their reports affect the way foods are processed, textiles are manufactured, clothing is constructed, houses are built, and products for the home are developed and used.

[10

Try It Out

Read a research report in the *Journal of Home Economics* on some aspect of home economics that is of interest to you. Prepare a summary of the article covering these points: What information did the researcher want to obtain from the research project? What method did he or she use? What equipment was used in the research? What conclusions were reached? What evidence supports the conclusions? How can the conclusions be applied to everyday life?

THE CAREER:
EXTENSION SERVICE WORKER

A graduate home economist with a major in home economics education may become an extension worker. Extension home economists are employed by certain colleges and the United States Department of Agriculture, in cooperation with the local county in which they work. Their job is to bring homemaking information to men and women who are no longer in school. They teach in community centers, health centers, churches and temples, and in people's homes. Their subjects include nutrition, buying and preparing foods, managing family income, bringing up children, keeping healthy—and anything else related to the needs and wants of the people in the area. They also train members of 4-H clubs, aged ten to twenty-one, in new homemaking skills. Through classes, workshops, meetings, bulletins, newsletters, TV and radio appearances, and home visits, the extension home economist helps to bring information to the public in a way that is easy to understand and to apply to their lives.

Extension home economists use information that they gather from other professionals in the community,

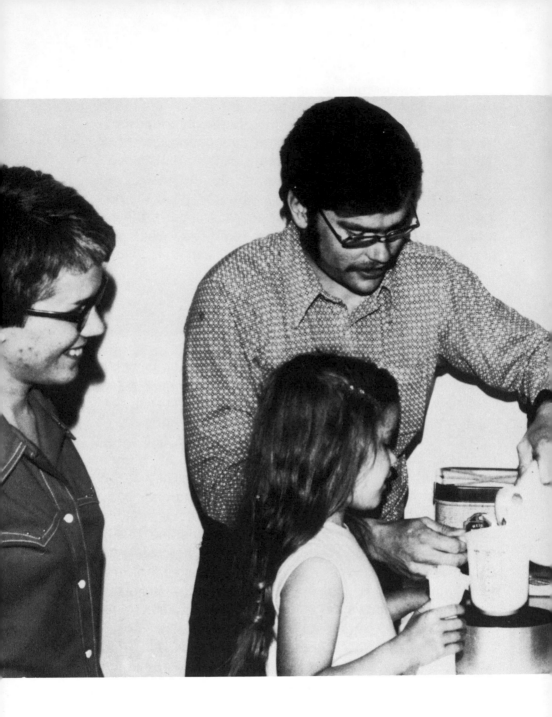

**Extension home economist (left)
helps this single parent learn how to
prepare nourishing meals for his family.**

such as health workers and social workers, to guide them in planning programs and preparing materials. From farm towns to urban slums, home economists in the Extension Service help people by locating and training those in the community who have special abilities, in cooking, sewing, home decorating, nutrition, or recreation, to teach their skills to others. The home economist who works for the Extension Service reaches many, many people by training leaders to train others in homemaking.

Try It Out

Find out how the needs of the older citizens in your community are being met. Compile a list of services to the aged that are offered by senior citizens centers, adult education programs, schools, hospitals, community recreation centers, housing developments, or other institutions. Prepare a flyer to display in your local library that presents your findings. Based on your investigation, do you think there is a need in your community for additional services for the elderly?

THE CAREER:
CONSUMER EDUCATOR

Many local, state, and federal consumer affairs offices, banks, utilities, insurance companies, and finance companies employ home economists for their consumer education programs. These consumer educators prepare printed materials, give courses, talks or demonstrations, answer questions and letters, and advise customers.

Consumer educators are found in every area of home economics. Those with a background in food and nutrition are hired by food manufacturers and processors, and government agencies such as the Food and

**Consumers are shown
how to can food
safely and economically.**

Drug Administration, the Department of Agriculture, and the Peace Corps. Those who are strong in science often work for consumer-testing organizations. Those who specialize in fabrics, home furnishings, and equipment are employed by the large clothing, furniture, or appliance manufacturers or retailers. Those who are trained in art, publicity, writing, or photography work in a variety of advertising or public relations positions in business, industry, or government.

Try It Out

Research and write an article on Bicycle Safety —Do's and Don'ts. Include information on things to look for when purchasing a bicycle, and hints on caring for and repairing bicycles. For recent safety information on bicycles, write to the Consumer Product Safety Commission (Bureau of Information and Education, Washington, D.C. 20207), and consult *Consumer Reports* and *Consumers' Research Magazine.* Submit your article to the school newspaper for possible publication.

REQUIREMENTS

To become a junior or senior high school home economics teacher, or an extension worker, you need a four-year college bachelor's degree in home economics education. College and university teaching positions require at least a master's degree, which takes one to two years beyond the bachelor's degree. More often, a Doctor of Philosophy degree is needed, which takes an additional two or three years. A bachelor's degree in home economics or in liberal arts, with a major in home economics, is needed for many government or business positions in the field of consumer education.

To work as a clerk or a secretary in a consumer education or consumer affairs office, you need a high school diploma, preferably with courses in home economics, as well as a certain amount of office skills.

SALARY POTENTIAL

Junior and senior high school teacher	$ 7,000 to $20,000
College and university teacher	$12,000 to $25,000
Research assistant	$14,000 to $16,000
Extension home economist	$ 9,000 to $20,000
Consumer educator	$ 8,000 to $12,000
Education materials writer	$ 9,000 to $15,000

START NOW

Join the Future Homemakers of America through your home economics teacher, and become an active member.

Volunteer to work in your local consumer affairs office or Extension Service office.

Read *Co-ed* magazine (for students) or *Journal of Home Economics* (for teachers of home economics).

Join a consumer group in your area. For a list of such organizations, write to:

National Consumers League
1785 Massachusetts Ave., NW
Washington, D.C. 20036

Consumers' Association of Canada
251 Laurier Ave. W. #801
Ottawa, Canada K1P 527

For more information on careers in home economics education, write to:
American Home Economics Association
2010 Massachusetts Ave., NW
Washington, D.C. 20036

Home Economics Education Association
1201 16th St., NW
Washington, D.C. 20036

Canadian Home Economics Association
409A Burnside Building, 151 Slater St.
Ottawa, Canada KIP 5H3

Extension Service
Department of Agriculture
Washington, D.C. 20250

Child Development
and Family Relations

The way children grow and develop depends on two factors—heredity and environment. Heredity is the inborn set of characteristics that is passed on from parents to children. Environment refers to the surroundings that shape individuals and determine how they will use their inherited abilities.

If the environment includes good medical care and nutritious, well-balanced meals, children are helped to develop well physically. If it includes parents who talk to them, play with them, and show them love and tenderness, they are helped to develop well psychologically, socially, and emotionally. And if it includes books and toys, music and art, and a wide range of experiences, they are helped to develop well intellectually.

It is the work of home economists who specialize in child development and family relations to help to improve the environment of young children by teaching and training the children, and by guiding and counseling their parents.

[18

THE CAREER:
TEACHER OR
YOUTH WORKER

Home economists trained in child development work with children of different ages in a variety of educational settings. The nursery school teacher may work in a private nursery school, a parents' cooperative nursery, a Head Start program, or a day-care center. The teacher creates a relaxed atmosphere for the preschoolers, who are usually between the ages of two and a half and five. They help the children learn to play with others, share, take turns, and be kind to one another. They guide the youngsters through a daily routine of playing, eating, and resting. They provide experiences that include moving and listening to music, experimenting with art materials, building with blocks, and playing with other indoor and outdoor toys and equipment.

The teacher of handicapped children—the blind, deaf, mentally retarded, emotionally disturbed, or physically disabled—works either in a school for exceptional children or in a school that serves all children. These teachers cover many of the same subjects that are taught in regular classrooms. But they give these students with special needs a great deal of extra help in overcoming their handicaps, so that they may function as well as they can and lead useful, satisfying lives.

The community youth-worker organizes and leads social and recreational activities for boys and girls of school age. Many of these programs are under the auspices of after-school programs, of scouts, 4-H clubs, Y's, church and temple groups, or other types of community organizations. Youth workers hire trained leaders, teachers, and performers to present and supervise various activities. They make facilities available for parties, dances, sports, classes, shows, and performances.

And they plan for camping and hiking trips, bicycle tours, attendance at concerts, shows and sporting events, and other activities that fit the needs and interests of their groups.

All successful nursery school teachers, teachers of the handicapped, and community youth-workers enjoy being with children and show a healthy respect for them as people. They know what to expect from the youngsters according to their age and ability. Good teachers and youth workers are relaxed and friendly, fair and flexible in their teaching methods and approach. Their goal is to bring out the best in every individual. Their instruction, guidance, and the varied experiences that they provide are designed to broaden the children's understanding of themselves and of the world in which they live.

Try It Out

Write a short children's story that you think would be interesting to children in a nursery school. Make a set of drawings to illustrate the story. Find a local nursery school, day-care center, or Head Start program, and ask permission to read your story to the youngsters. Watch carefully for their reactions to learn which parts they like, which parts they do not like, and which parts they do not understand. At the end of the reading, ask questions and judge their responses. Then rewrite the story and read it again, to the same or to a different group. If the children and the teacher are enthusiastic about the story, you could ask your librarian for the names and addresses of children's magazines that might be interested in publishing it.

THE CAREER:
SOCIAL WORKER

Home economists trained in child development and

family relations may become social workers. Social workers are employed by government or private welfare agencies, community development centers, family-aid bureaus, hospitals, and schools. They try to help people in need to work out and solve their problems. A bedridden mother cannot care for her young children; a child is truant from school because she is ashamed of the clothes that she has to wear; a wife is fearful because she is being threatened by her husband from whom she is separated; a teen-aged son has run away from home, and threatens to run away again. These are some of the problems that social workers or welfare home economists encounter—and try to solve—from day to day.

Whenever possible, the social workers arrange for help from their own agencies. This help may take the form of welfare payments, household help, psychological counseling, temporary housing, or donations of food or clothing. If they cannot provide relief, the social workers advise and suggest other sources for help and assistance.

Social workers get great personal satisfaction from helping others to solve their problems and making it possible for people to live with dignity and pleasure. Through their work with families and individuals, social workers contribute to improving the well-being of the whole community.

Try It Out

Obtain a list of social service and welfare agencies in your community or town. In the following three situations, name an agency that might help, the aid that it could provide, other possible sources of help, and the likely outcome of the situation:

1. Amy is a seventeen-year-old high school senior. She has just learned that she has a serious kidney disease that requires weekly treatments. The treat-

**A social worker leads a
discussion group for senior citizens.**

ments are very expensive and her family cannot afford to pay for them, even though both of her parents are working.

2. Mrs. Brooks is a sixty-eight-year-old widow, living alone, who fell and broke her hip several months ago. She is home now from the hospital, but cannot get around well enough to take care of herself, nor does she want to enter a nursing home.
3. Mrs. Johnson abandoned her husband and three children ranging in age from six months to just over three years. Mr. Johnson cannot keep his present job and care for the children at the same time.

REQUIREMENTS

Most teachers, youth workers, and social workers require at least a four-year bachelor's degree and field-work experience in their field. Their courses may include a background in home economics, psychology, human development, and parent education.

High school graduates with home economics courses that emphasize child care may find work as paraprofessionals or aides in a day-care center, Head Start program, nursery school, kindergarten, or school for handicapped children. They may assist in community centers, hospitals, playgrounds, and children's homes. There are also some limited opportunities for social-work aides or assistants in social-service agencies.

SALARY POTENTIAL

Nursery school or Head Start teacher	$ 6,000 to $ 9,500
Elementary school teacher or teacher of the handicapped	$ 6,000 to $16,000
Teacher's aides	$ 4.00 per hour

Community youth worker	$ 9,000 to $12,500
Social worker	$12,000 to $18,000
Welfare home economist	$12,000 to $14,000

START NOW

If you like working with young children, volunteer as an assistant in a nursery school, a Head Start program, or a day-care center.

If you prefer school-aged children, become active in a scout group, a Y, a 4-H club, a community center, or an after-school program.

If you are thinking of a career in social work, volunteer to work in a hospital, nursing home, or similar institution. Look for opportunities to talk to the patients, get to know their problems, and see if there are some ways in which you might help.

Read *Childhood Education, Journal of Marriage and the Family,* and *Parents' Magazine* for interesting articles that relate to teaching and raising children.

Write to these professional organizations if you wish specific career information on opportunities in the field of child care:

Day Care and Child Development Council of America
1012 14th St., NW
Washington, D.C. 20005

National Association for the Education of Young
  Children
1834 Connecticut Ave., NW
Washington, D.C. 20009

Association for Early Childhood Education
55 Charles E., Apt. 703
Toronto, Canada M4Y 1S9

Write to the following for information on social work:

National Association of Social Workers
1425 H St., NW
Washington, D.C. 20005

Canadian Association of Social Workers
Ste. 400, 55 Parkdale Ave.
Ottawa, Canada K1Y 1E5

Food and Nutrition

Every man and woman trained in the food and nutrition area of home economics understands that food is of vital importance to the health and welfare of all people. Some teach others the basics of food and nutrition, so that they can eat correctly and meet their own nutritional needs. Some use their basic knowledge of food nutrients and the way food affects growth and development to plan diets and make up menus. And some encourage good eating by preparing and serving well-balanced meals to large numbers of people in an attractive, appealing, and appetizing way.

THE CAREER:
NUTRITIONIST

Nutritionists raise the level of health in a community by teaching and doing research on the science of food and the principles of nutrition. They lecture, advise, consult, and guide people in what to eat for good health. A nutritionist may meet with a group of expectant moth-

This cafeteria serves nutritious food to its elderly patrons.

ers in the morning, visit a school and talk to a group of teachers and nurses on the eating problems of young children in the afternoon, and work with adolescents in an obesity clinic in the evening. Working with all ages, with all income levels, and with all conditions of health, from the chronically ill to the healthy, nutritionists care about people and are able to provide their services to individuals of all backgrounds.

Nutritionists should speak and write clearly, so that they can get their ideas across effectively. Well-groomed and healthy, nutritionists should look as though they practice what they preach. And they should have the patience, tact, and adjustability to work well with different people in different situations.

Try It Out

Compare the nutritional value of yogurt and milk. Use the nutritional labels on the containers as your source of nutritional information. Compare the number of calories; the amount of protein, vitamins, and minerals. Can you come to a conclusion as to which is the more nutritious food? Compare the prices to decide which is the less expensive source of nutrients. Will your findings change the amounts of milk and yogurt that you eat?

THE CAREER: DIETITIAN

The work of the dietitian is a little different from the work of the nutritionist. Dietitians feed people, rather than teach them about nutrition or do research with food. More dietitians work in hospitals, nursing homes, and similar institutions than anywhere else.

Usually a dietitian is in charge of the hospital or nursing home kitchen and is responsible for supervising the buying and preparation of the food. The dietitian knows how to balance menus and select special foods for people recovering from various illnesses, before and after major surgery, and for the chronically ill. Often the dietitian tours the hospital and talks to doctors and nurses to see how well the patients are doing, and how their diets might be adjusted to speed their recovery.

Science is an important part of every dietitian's training. But they are also interested in the way food looks and tastes. Dietitians know that food that is attractive in appearance and is well served will be more appealing to the patients.

Try It Out

The Department of Agriculture has developed a Daily Food Plan based on four food groups—milk, cheese, and ice cream; meat, fish, poultry, and eggs; vegetables and fruit; breads, cereal, and spaghetti. They recommend two to four servings from each group every day.

Plan a one-week menu for a family following the Daily Food Plan. Try to include as much variety as possible; do not repeat any main dish.

THE CAREER:
FOOD SERVICE MANAGER

Some home economists who specialize in dietetics and nutrition become food service managers. They find employment in the cafeterias and dining rooms of schools and colleges, factories, hotels, airports, and other places where large numbers of people are fed. Their job is to plan the menus and to supervise the buying, preparing, and serving of the food.

Food service managers are trained to do even more. They frequently plan and equip kitchens, even choosing

**Food service manager
and chef plan the menu.**

the pots and pans. They hire and supervise the employees. They keep records on the expenses of running the food service. Successful food service managers combine a thorough knowledge of all aspects of food preparation with a good head for business.

Try It Out

Plan a menu for a birthday party for forty boys and girls to cost less than fifty dollars. What foods would you serve? How much of each food would you need to buy? List the utensils or appliances that you would need for cooking or preparing the food. List the serving pieces and dishes that you would require for serving the food. List the items you would need to set the table. What would you use for the centerpiece?

Estimate the cost of each item on your list that you would need to buy, and total the amount. Is the total less than fifty dollars? If not, how could you trim your costs?

REQUIREMENTS

A minimum requirement for a career as a nutritionist, dietitian, or food service manager is a bachelor's degree. To advance in the field, though, a master's degree is usually needed. A good many nutritionists go on to earn a doctor's degree, either a Ph.D. (Doctor of Philosophy) or an M.D. (Doctor of Medicine).

Paraprofessionals with a high school diploma can enter the field as a school lunchroom aide, kitchen helper, waiter or waitress, food demonstrator, or caterer's assistant. A high school graduate with a background in home economics can also become a cook, chef, baker, food technician or technologist, or even the manager of a small restaurant or other food establishment.

SALARY POTENTIAL

Public health nutritionist	$10,000 to $20,000
Hospital dietitian	$11,000 to $20,000
Nutrition or dietetic aide	$ 6,000 to $10,000
Food service manager	$14,000 to $18,000
Food service technician	$ 7,500 to $10,000
Chef	$14,000 to $30,000

START NOW

Plan the menu and shop, cook, and serve meals for your family from time to time.

Try to get a job in the kitchen or dining room of a luncheonette, restaurant, summer camp, or resort hotel. Perhaps you can find work in a retail food establishment such as a supermarket, bakery, or grocery store.

Become a volunteer in a hospital, nursing home, or other institution, and ask to be assigned to the food service.

Start a home-catering service or baking business for church groups or social clubs in your neighborhood.

Read *FDA Consumer, Food Technology, Journal of the American Dietetic Association,* and *The Journal of Nutrition* to learn about the various phases of food science and technology, ways to increase the world's food supply, and new methods of preparing and serving food.

For information on nutrition, dietetics, and food-service training after high school, write to:

American Dietetic Association
430 N. Michigan Ave.
Chicago, Ill. 60611

American Institute of Nutrition
9650 Rockville Pike
Bethesda, Md. 20014

Food and Drug Administration
5600 Fishers Lane
Rockville, Md. 20852

Institute of Food Technologists
221 North LaSalle St.
Chicago, Ill. 60601

Council on Hotel, and Restaurant, and Institu-
tional Education
11 Koger Executive Center, Ste. 219
Norfolk, Va. 23501

Canadian Institute of Food Science and Technology
Ste. 10, 46 Elgin Street
Ottawa, Canada K1P 5K6

Clothing and Textiles

The world of fashion can be exciting and glamorous. From selecting the bolt of cloth to designing the garment, from cutting the pattern to sewing it all together, from modeling the article to advertising it in magazines and newspapers—the work of home economists in textiles and clothing offers many career opportunities.

THE CAREER:
FASHION DESIGNER

Every article of clothing begins with an idea for something different or new that will be useful, appealing, and attractive. Fashion designers create the styles for new garments and accessories, and new patterns for fabrics. Many fashion designers are home economists who specialize in the field of clothing and textiles.

Fashion designers combine an interest in clothing with a talent in art. They notice the ways different groups of people dress and the clothes that they wear in differ-

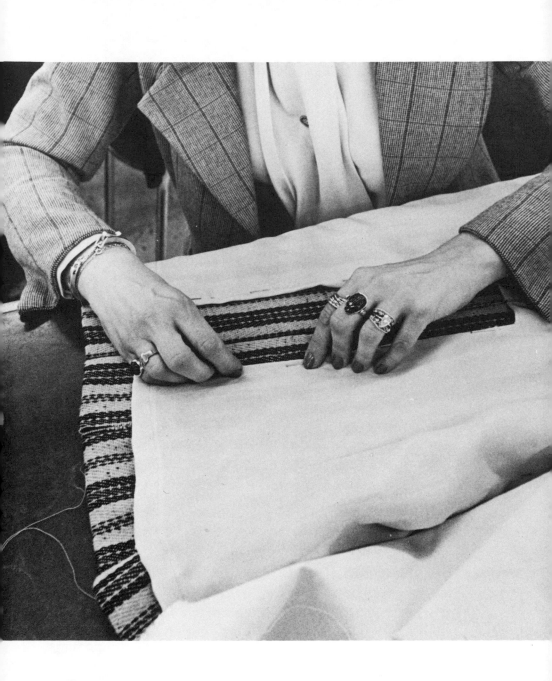

**Fashion designers combine
an interest in clothing with a
talent for artistic expression.**

ent situations and for different activities. They are sensitive to style and what makes one outfit more attractive and practical than another. They have a sense of what colors, textures, and patterns go well together.

Designers know all about the different fabrics—wool, cotton, synthetics, and blends. They can tell which fabrics are suitable for which garments. They can predict how an article of clothing will look and how comfortable it will be when it is worn.

"Tuned in" to the latest styles, designers are aware of current trends in formal wear, sportswear, and casual, everyday clothes. They like to handle beautiful materials, enjoy using their imagination to create new clothing, and are able to apply practical judgment to the construction of clothing for people of all ages.

Try It Out

Create a top or vest for yourself or a friend out of an old, long-sleeved shirt. Look at pictures in fashion magazines, in pattern books, or even in the encyclopedia at costumes of people in other cultures for inspiration. Sketch your ideas on pieces of paper. Then cut and sew the old shirt until you have made something new and original and wearable out of it.

THE CAREER:
GARMENT WORKER

The mass production of clothes—dresses, suits, coats, hats, accessories—takes place in clothing facto-

Garment workers
can be men as
well as women.

**Pattern cutters are an essential
part of the garment industry.**

ries. Many different kinds of workers, some trained in home economics, are employed in this industry. Pattern-makers prepare the master patterns from the original design. They figure out how the garment will be cut and put together. Assistants to the patternmakers, called graders, add marks for darts, hems, buttons, buttonholes, and pockets to the basic pattern. The cutters decide the best way to position the master pattern to use efficiently every inch of the fabric. They spread many layers of cloth on the long cutting table and by machine cut out hundreds of identical pieces of fabric at one time. These pieces go to the sewing machine operators who sew the separate pieces into complete garments. The pressers use large steam irons to make the garment smooth and neat. And finally, the finishers add the decorations, such as buttons and snaps, that complete the article of clothing.

Custom-made garments and boutique-type items—handwoven apparel, bridal gowns and accessories, hand-sewn clothing, handmade dolls and toys—also utilize knowledge and skill in cutting, putting together, fitting, and finishing. Many of these hand-sewers, tailors, and fitters work in their own businesses or in the alterations department of small shops or department stores.

Business, industry, the mass media, and government employ home economists who have a broad knowledge of clothing and textiles to work in many settings, from laboratories, where they test fabrics and items of apparel, to classrooms, where they instruct homemakers on the care of clothing and on clothing construction.

Try It Out

Make yourself something to wear by following the directions in a pattern that you select. Choose a simple design to begin with. Buy enough fabric for your size. Pin the pattern to the fabric and cut the garment according to the cutting guides. Follow instructions for marking, basting, and fitting. Stitch and press as you go along. Finish details and give the slacks, blouse, shirt, or other apparel a final pressing before you wear it.

THE CAREER:
CLOTHING SALESPERSON
AND CLOTHING BUYER

Most clothing factories employ a sales force to sell the clothes they produce to department stores, small shops, and mail-order houses. These employees know all the different garments that are produced by the factory. They try to convince the representatives of retail stores to buy their line of merchandise. Some of these salespeople work at the factory and sell the clothes from there. Others travel around visiting individual stores in different towns and cities.

Many stores employ buyers who either go to the factories or see visiting salespeople in the stores. Buyers choose and select from among all the styles made by the different factories. They decide which ones their customers will like. Over and over again they make decisions about which clothes are of the best quality, the best style and color, and in the right price range. They are careful to order enough garments to meet the expected demand, but not so many that there will be leftovers at the end of the season.

Successful buyers also understand the economics of the business. They ask themselves such questions as: What is this garment worth? What is the most I am willing to pay for it? Can I get a similar garment at a lower price elsewhere? Can I sell it at a price that is low enough to meet the competition, and yet high enough to make a profit for the store?

Placing the order is just the first step. The buyers

have to follow through and make sure that the order is filled correctly, that everything arrives on schedule, and in good condition. Then they follow the sales reports. If the item sells very well, they may need to place another order. From the sales figures, too, they learn what is selling best and what is not selling at all. Their awareness of buying trends influences their future buying habits.

Both factory salespeople and department store buyers enjoy selecting and handling merchandise. They are "up" on the latest fabrics and the latest styles and trends in fashion. They dress attractively and are very well groomed. They enjoy meeting and talking to people and can quickly tell what their customers will admire and buy.

Try It Out

Plan a complete wardrobe for someone who is going off to college. Think of typical college activities, such as classes, sports and recreation, evening dates and parties, and so on. Decide what special clothes are needed for each activity. Try to work out outfits that can be worn for more than one purpose and can be combined with other outfits for variety.

Go to a local department store and find out the prices for the items in your planned wardrobe. How much does the entire outfit cost? What items could most easily be left out if you had to cut the cost by one-quarter? by one-half?

THE CAREER:
FASHION COPYWRITER, ILLUSTRATOR, AND PHOTOGRAPHER

The advertising departments of clothing stores and factories employ writers, artists, and photographers to plan and carry out programs that inform people about their goods and attract customers to their merchandise. Copywriters prepare the texts for the ads. They find the catchy words and clever descriptions that make the readers notice the message.

Fashion illustrators and photographers prepare the pictures for the ads. They try to show the clothes in the most appealing and attention-getting ways. They often work with models wearing the outfits they are trying to promote. Layout artists put the text and pictures together to create the finished ad. They adapt the ads to fit into the styles of different magazines and newspapers.

Try It Out

Cut out a full-page fashion ad from a newspaper or magazine. Go over the text very carefully. Then rewrite the text, trying to make it more interesting or more attractive. Look at the photo or drawing. Can you think of ways to improve the picture? Make a sketch of your idea. Is there any way you might make the layout better? On a blank piece of paper, sketch your new layout, and insert any text or picture changes.

Compare your result with the printed ad. Is yours better? Why? Is the printed ad better? Why?

REQUIREMENTS

If you are interested in a career in this field, you may attend a four-year college that offers home economics courses, along with courses in textiles and fabrics, art and design, costume, marketing, fashion mer-

These students are perfecting their skills in fashion illustration.

chandising, and accounting. Many two-year community colleges also offer special programs in clothing and textiles.

It is easier to become a wholesale or retail salesperson, a demonstrator of sewing or sewing machines, or any one of many related positions if you have a high school diploma and have taken one or more home economics courses.

SALARY POTENTIAL

Fashion designer	$10,000 to $30,000
Sewing machine operator	$ 6,000 to $ 8,000
Wholesale salesperson	$10,000 to $18,000
Retail buyer	$12,000 to $19,000
Assistant buyer	$ 8,000 to $10,500
Fashion copywriter, illustrator, or photographer	$ 7,500 to $22,000

START NOW

Try to get a summer or part-time job in a clothing factory or store, in a laundry or dry cleaning plant, or in a fabric store. Be alert to what the different workers are doing, and try to learn about the various jobs and duties.

Visit a trade or technical school, or a college, where people are being trained in designing, weaving, manufacturing, or advertising textiles and clothing.

Read fashion magazines, such as *Vogue, Glamour, Seventeen, Mademoiselle,* and *Harper's Bazaar,* to keep up with new styles; and trade journals such as *Women's Wear Daily* and *Modern Textiles Magazine,* to get an insider's view of the clothing and textile industry.

For more information on careers for home economists in clothing and textiles, write to:

[44

International Association of Clothing Designers
12 South 12th St.
Philadelphia, Pa. 19107

Textile Industry Product Safety Committee
1750 Pennsylvania Ave., NW
Washington, D.C. 20006

Canadian Textiles Institute
Ste. 1002, 1080 Beaver Hall Hill
Montreal, Canada H2Z 1T6

Housing, Home Furnishings, and Equipment

A house is much more than a place to hang your hat. A house is where you can find comfort and safety, privacy and pleasure. Home economists who specialize in housing, home furnishings, and equipment help families to get the best possible housing they can afford. They give advice on housing and on the construction of homes. Others plan and design the interiors. Some suggest the appliances and equipment that will make housekeeping easier and more convenient.

THE CAREER: HOUSING SPECIALIST

Some home economists who are housing specialists are hired as consultants, either by home builders or by individuals buying new homes. These professionals know the local zoning and building laws, as well as the required electrical and plumbing standards. This information is vital both to the builder and to the buyer, since it is a guarantee that the house will be safely and well built and will meet all of the legal requirements.

The housing specialists oversee the design of the house and make sure that the proper materials and construction methods are used. They select equipment, such as the heating and air-conditioning systems; and major appliances, such as stove, sinks, and refrigerator. They give advice on organizing the interior of the house to make the most efficient use of the space.

Housing specialists do not only work with new houses. They are also hired as consultants when older homes are remodeled or rebuilt. They are sometimes called in to help with larger construction projects, such as government or industrial buildings. Other jobs include giving advice on how to adapt buildings for the aged or for the physically handicapped, and preparing information or educational material related to housing.

Specialists in housing know that people feel better about themselves, and act better toward others, when they live comfortably in well-constructed houses and in nice neighborhoods. Crime, disease, and juvenile delinquency are often by-products of run-down, unsanitary, segregated, and overcrowded housing. Housing specialists want to provide pleasant surroundings for others. They are interested in people's welfare and are able to work well with a variety of people having a variety of tastes.

Try It Out

Find ads in your local newspaper for houses or apartments that are available and suitable for a young couple with two very little children. What is the average price of a small home? What is the average monthly rental of two- or three-bedroom apartments? What information would you need to have in order to find accommodations for the couple? What are the advantages and disadvantages of apartments? of private homes?

THE CAREER:
INTERIOR DESIGNER

Home economists who are trained as interior designers plan, select, buy, and arrange the furniture, wall decorations, floor coverings, upholstery, and accessories in new homes, or homes that are being redecorated. Many are in business for themselves; some work in large department stores or home furnishings stores. Besides working for individuals and families, they may also work for construction firms, hotels, restaurants, and industrial firms that produce home furnishings.

Designers talk to clients to collect information on the space to be decorated; the client's needs, desires, and tastes; and the amount of money that can be spent. With the wishes of the client in mind, the designer prepares a written design plan that is based on his or her training in good housing and knowledge of home furnishings.

The designer and client go over the plan and make changes and adjustments until both are satisfied. Next, the designer fills in the details of the plan—the exact models and styles of the furniture, the fabric coverings, the decorations, and so on.

Once again, the designer and the client talk and reach an agreement on the details. The designer now places the orders for the furnishings and takes the nec-

**Interior designers
create pleasant,
practical rooms
for every purpose.**

essary steps to prepare the house, schedule the deliveries, receive and check all shipments, and see that all furnishings are properly placed and installed. The goal of the interior designer is to achieve a comfortable, efficient home, at a cost within the original budget. The reward is the satisfaction and pride of completing a job well done.

Try It Out

Stand in the doorway of your room and draw a floor plan on a piece of graph paper. Show all the furniture (bed, desk, dresser, lamp, rug) in the room. Place a piece of tracing paper over the drawing and copy the outlines of the furnishings. Color the objects in the room various shades of red, orange, and pink. How does that color scheme work? On another piece of tracing paper, outline the same objects, but color them using a blue, green, and yellow color scheme. Which scheme do you like better? How do the different color combinations change the appearance of the room?

THE CAREER:
HOME EQUIPMENT DEMONSTRATOR

Each year, many new kinds of household products come on the market. There are microwave ovens, no-frost refrigerators, toaster-broiler oven combinations, cordless vacuum cleaners, and electric slow-cooking pots. Each item is designed to be an improvement over an older household item. They are designed to save the homemaker work and time by making some homemaking tasks easier and faster.

The manufacturers and distributors of these appliances hire home economists, sometimes called home service representatives, to demonstrate and instruct

**This home economist is demonstrating
how to use an electric bread kneader.**

consumers on how to use the new equipment. They want to make sure that the equipment is used correctly, to encourage sales and to ensure customer satisfaction. These home economists are a link between the manufacturers and the consumers.

Home economists who specialize in this field are knowledgeable about the latest in home appliances and equipment. They are outgoing people, who can talk easily to individuals or to large groups. They are just as comfortable giving a cooking demonstration to a few people in a department store as they are demonstrating a new type of dishwasher on coast-to-coast television.

Try It Out

Research the subject of air-conditioners. Find out the scientific principle on which they work. List the factors to consider when buying an air-conditioner. What are the special features that the consumer should look for? What are the chief differences among different brands of air-conditioners? Check the ratings on air-conditioners in *Consumer Reports* and *Consumers' Research Magazine.* What features do they focus on in their evaluations? Do their reports confirm what your own research has uncovered?

REQUIREMENTS

Most home economists in this field have at least a bachelor's degree, with a major in their specialty. With a high school diploma, a graduate may work in a furniture factory or with a construction company, assist in a landscaping firm, sell real estate or home furnishings, work in an upholstery or painting business, or install or repair appliances.

SALARY POTENTIAL

Housing consultant	$12,000 to $17,500
Home furnishings designer	$17,000 to $21,000
Interior designer	$ 6,000 to $12,000
Home furnishings salesperson	$ 7,500 to $10,000
Home equipment demonstrator	$ 6,000 to $11,500

START NOW

Try to get a summer or part-time job in a furniture or appliance store, an interior designer's office, or architect's office. Perhaps you can work as a helper to a plumber, a carpenter, an electrician, a gardener, or a painter.

Read the magazines that deal with the home, such as *American Home, Better Homes and Gardens, Good Housekeeping, Interior Design*—and the publication of the industry, *Home Furnishings Daily*.

For further information on careers in interior design and home service, write to:

American Society of Interior Designers
730 Fifth Ave.
New York, N.Y. 10019

National Home Furnishings Association
1150 Merchandise Mart Plaza
Chicago, Ill. 60654

Interior Designers of Canada
302-1008 Homer Street
Vancouver, British Columbia, Canada V6B 2X1

Family Finance and Home Management

Managing money is a problem for many people. Every day, decisions have to be made on how much to spend on food, clothing, housing, medical care, education, recreation, insurance—and how much to save. Some families, particularly those with limited incomes, have difficulty living within their means. They are involved in a never-ending struggle to stay ahead of the bill collectors. Other families lose the struggle and reach a point of financial collapse.

A good number of families are now turning to professionals in family finance for help and suggestions on how to handle their incomes and run their homes. These specialists in finance and home management offer information and advice that make it possible for these families to achieve financial security and to lead happier and more satisfying lives.

THE CAREER:
FINANCE AND
MANAGEMENT SPECIALIST

The work of the home economist who specializes in finance is primarily education, even though these specialists work in government welfare offices, charitable organizations, or hospitals, rather than schools. Sometimes called welfare home economists or extension specialists in family economics, they guide families in setting up realistic budgets that balance income and expenses. They give advice on how to achieve the goals of the budget. They set up home management standards, planning for the costs of the various items necessary in a home. They prepare schedules of money allowances for low-income families. They assist families in caring for a member who is sick or handicapped. They provide immediate aid for those who face a financial emergency.

Home economists who specialize in this field may also find employment in business. They can work for banks, loan companies, insurance companies, investment houses, finance corporations, utilities, and department stores. They answer questions on saving, budgeting, and investing. They prepare materials that encourage people to save more, invest more, or use credit more wisely. Also, they write financial columns in newspapers and magazines. In talks before clubs, social organizations, on radio and TV, they give people advice on how to control and direct their finances.

Many institutions that house large numbers of people also employ these home economist specialists to be homemakers on a very large scale. College dormitories, child-care institutions, hotels and resorts, clubs, hospitals, and nursing homes hire home managers, who are called executive housekeepers. A person in this position

**Finance specialists help
people plan present
and future budgets.**

knows everything about maintaining the health, safety, and comfort of a large number of people who live together. His or her responsibilities range from preparing annual budgets to knowing how many bars of soap to order at one time, from hiring and firing personnel to arranging the furniture in the lobby.

Working as a home-management or finance specialist requires a good understanding of business and economics. Also, the worker needs an ability to communicate well with others and to win people's confidence, so that they speak honestly and are willing to accept suggestions. As in other fields of home economics, the specialists are able to set aside their own personal attitudes to better serve others.

Try It Out

Many people do not earn enough money to meet all of their financial objectives. Below is a list of seven financial goals. Rewrite the list, placing the items in order, from the one that you give top priority to your item of lowest priority. Next to each item, write a sentence that explains your decision:
1. Having a car.
2. Having enough to eat.
3. Having insurance.
4. Owning nice clothes.
5. Owning your own home.
6. Investing in stocks and bonds.
7. Having savings in the bank.

REQUIREMENTS

Most home economists in the field of home management and family finance need a four-year college degree. Their courses include classes in home management and family finance, psychology, sociology, and economics, as well as in clothing and textiles, food and nutrition, and family relations.

The home economist who wishes to become an executive housekeeper, in addition to the general courses in home economics, takes courses in interior design, personnel management, purchasing, and accounting.

For high school graduates there are many opportunities in maintenance work, in building or institution services, and in jobs that combine maintenance and services. Child-care institutions, schools, hospitals, clinics and nursing homes, churches, libraries, museums, and recreation centers have such positions.

SALARY POTENTIAL

Welfare home economist	$12,000 to $14,000
Extension specialist in family economics	$ 9,000 to $14,000
Savings bank home economist	$10,000 to $18,000
Banker and life insurance representative	$10,000 to $25,000
Executive housekeeper	$ 7,000 to $21,000

START NOW

Keep records of the money you spend and the money you receive from allowances, and wages if you work. Analyze your spending habits. See if you can improve the way you spend your money.

Become more aware of family expenditures. See if you can spot strengths and weaknesses in the way your own family manages money.

Join or start a Youth Employment Service or place a Job Wanted ad in your local newspaper. Baby-sitting, tending a lawn, home repairs, painting, cleaning, or rubbish removal are good first-job opportunities.

Read *Business Week, Changing Times,* and *The Wall Street Journal* to become familiar with trends and terms in the world of business and finance.

For information on money management and facts you should know about borrowing, write to:

National Consumer Finance Association
1000 16th St., NW
Washington, D.C. 20036

Council of Better Business Bureaus
1150 17th St., NW
Washington, D.C. 20036

Association of Canadian Better Business Bureaux
Ste. 503, 71 Bank Street
Ottawa, Canada K1P 5N2

American Bankers Association
1120 Connecticut Ave., NW
Washington, D.C. 20036

Institute of Life Insurance
277 Park Ave
New York, N.Y. 10017

Index

About the Author

Gilda Berger is the possessor of many talents and interests. After receiving her bachelor's and master's degrees from the City University of New York, she put her special training to work by teaching exceptional children in the New York City, Long Beach, and Great Neck school systems. She is a strong believer in highly creative approaches to Special Education.

Somehow she has also found time to raise two daughters, write four children's books, and provide inestimable support to her author husband, Melvin Berger.

Gilda Berger lives with her family in Great Neck, New York, and is hard at work on her next book for Franklin Watts.